Hymns and Prayers for Children

Amsco Publications
New York / London / Sydney

Cover art direction by Mike Bell (UK)
Cover illustration by Graham Percy (UK)
Text illustrations by Kim Root (US)
Piano arrangements by Ronnie Ball (US)

All arrangements contained herein are
Copyright © 1985 by Amsco Music Publishing Company,
A Division of Music Sales Corporation, New York, NY.
This book published 1985 by Amsco Publications,
A Division of Music Sales Corporation, New York, NY.

Order No. AM 38639
US International Standard Book Number: 0.8256.0304.8

Exclusive Distributors:
Music Sales Corporation
257 Park Avenue South, New York, NY 10010 USA
Music Sales Limited
8/9 Frith Street, London W1V 5TZ England
Music Sales Pty. Limited
120 Rothschild Street, Rosebery, Sydney, NSW 2018, Australia

Printed in the United States of America by
Vicks Lithograph and Printing Corporation

1 Dear Lord & Father   2
2 Onward Christian Soldiers   3
3 Stand up, Stand up for Jesus   1
4 What a friend we have in Jesus.   4
5 There is a Green Hill far away   5

Abide With Me

1. A - bide with me: fast falls the e - ven - tide;
2. I need thy pres - ence ev - 'ry pass - ing hour;

The dark - ness deep - ens; Lord, with me a - bide;
What but thy grace can foil the tempt - er's pow'r?

When oth - er help - ers my fail, and com - forts flee,
Who like thy - self my guide and stay can be?

Help of the help-less, O a - bide with me.
Through cloud and sun-shine, O a - bide with me.

3. I fear no foe,
   with thee at hand to bless;
   Ill's have no weight,
   and tears no bitterness:
   Where is death's sting?
   where, grave, thy victory?
   I triumph still,
   if thou abide with me.

4. Hold thou thy cross
   before my closing eyes;
   Shine thro' the gloom,
   and point me to the skies:
   Heaven's morning breaks,
   and earth's vain shadows flee;
   In life, in death,
   O Lord, abide with me.

All People That On Earth Do Dwell

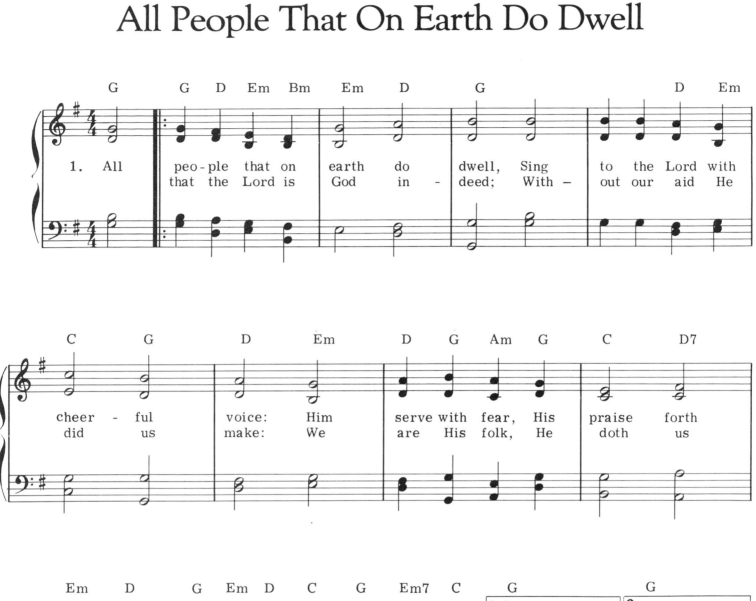

3. O enter than His gates with praise,

Approach with joy His courts unto;

Praise, laud, and bless His Name always,

For it is seemly so to do.

4. For why? the Lord our God is good,

His mercy is for ever sure;

His truth at all times firmly stood,

And shall from age to age endure.

All Things Bright And Beautiful

Refrain

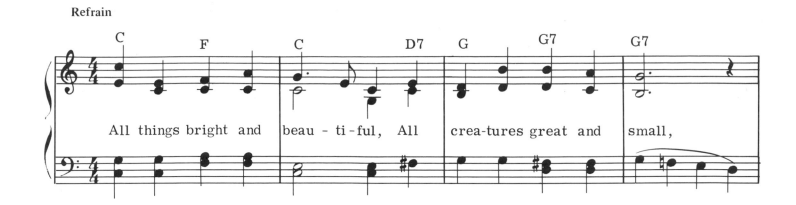

All things bright and beau - ti -ful, All crea-tures great and small,

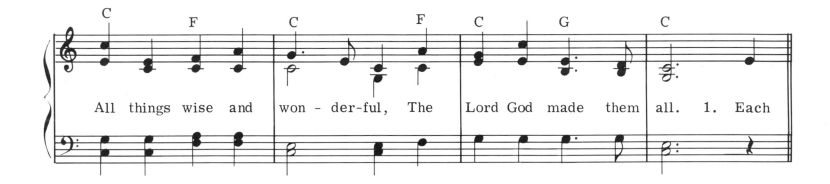

All things wise and won - der-ful, The Lord God made them all. 1. Each

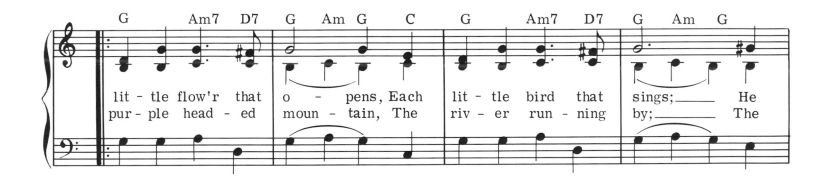

lit - tle flow'r that o — pens, Each lit - tle bird that sings;____ He
pur - ple head - ed moun - tain, The riv - er run - ning by;____ The

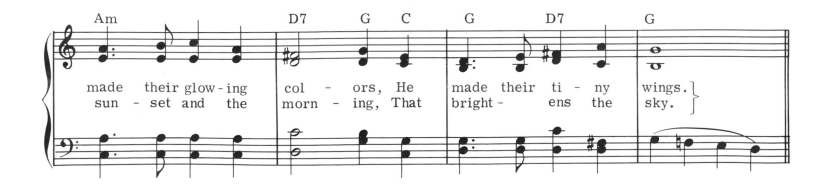

made their glow-ing col - ors, He made their ti - ny wings.
sun - set and the morn - ing, That bright - ens the sky.

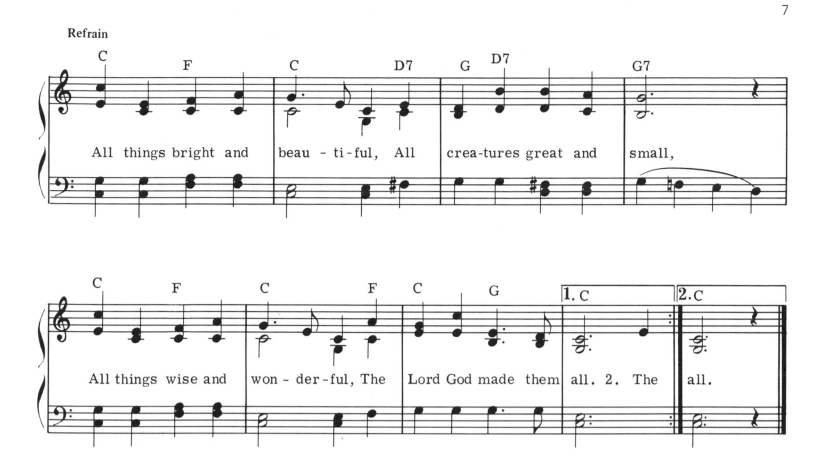

Refrain

C   F   C   D7   G   D7   G7

All things bright and beau – ti –ful, All crea-tures great and small,

C   F   C   F   C   G   1. C   2. C

All things wise and won – der –ful, The Lord God made them all. 2. The all.

3. The cold winter in the winter,
   The pleasant summer sun,
   The ripe fruits in the garden,
   He made them, ev'ry one:
      (Refrain)

4. The tall trees in the greenwood,
   The meadows where we play,
   The rushes by the water
   We gather ev'ry day:
      (Refrain)

5. He gave us eyes to see them,
   And lips that we might tell,
   How great is God Almighty,
   Who has made all things well:
      (Refrain)

Amazing Grace

1. A - maz - ing___ grace, how___ sweet the
2. grace that___ taught my___ heart to
3. we've been___ there ten___ thou - sand

sound that___ saved a___ wretch like me.___
fear and___ grace my___ fear re - lieved.___
years, bright shin - ing___ as the sun.___

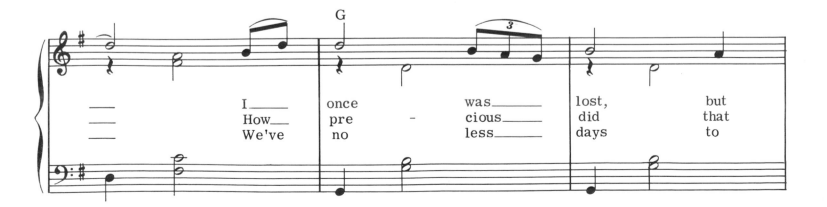

___ I___ once was___ lost, but
___ How___ pre - cious___ did that
___ We've no - less___ days to

now   am   found,   was____   blind   but
grace   ap   -   pear,   the____   hour   I
sing   God's   praise   than____   when   we

now   can   see.____   2. 'Twas
first   be - lieved.____   3. When
first   be - gun.____

Away In A Manger

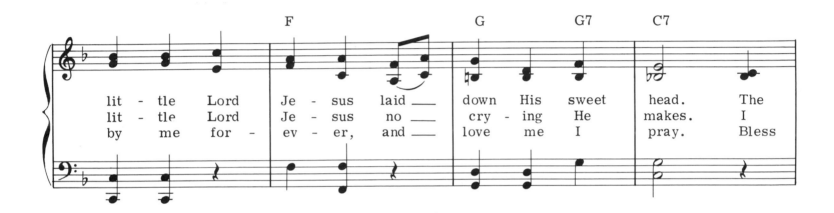

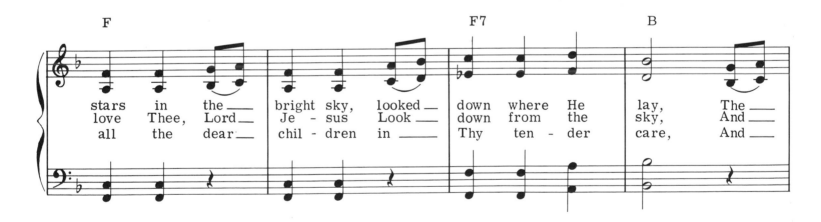

Can You Count The Stars?

Children Of The Heavenly King

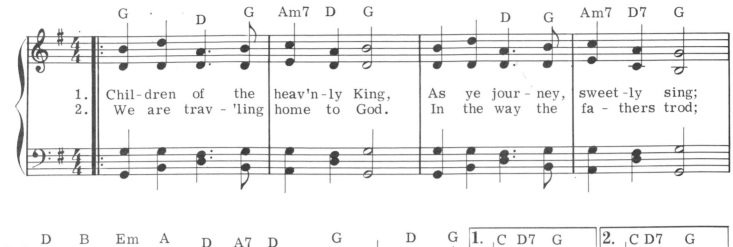

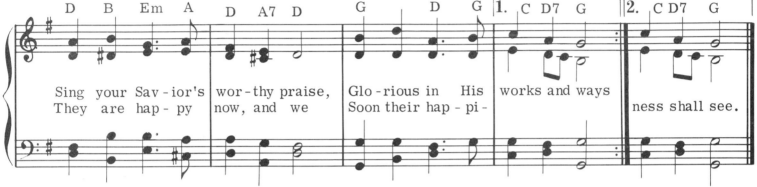

1. Chil-dren of the heav'n-ly King, As ye jour-ney, sweet-ly sing;
2. We are trav-'ling home to God. In the way the fa-thers trod;

Sing your Sav-ior's wor-thy praise, Glo-rious in His works and ways
They are hap-py now, and we Soon their hap-pi- ness shall see.

3. Lift your eyes, ye sons of light,
   Zion's city is in sight;
   There our endless home shall be,
   There our Lord we soon shall see.

4. Lord, obediently we go,
   Gladly leaving all below;
   Only Thou our leader be,
   And we still will follow Thee.

The Day Thou Gavest Lord Is Ended

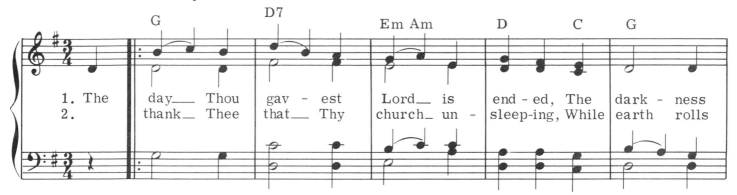

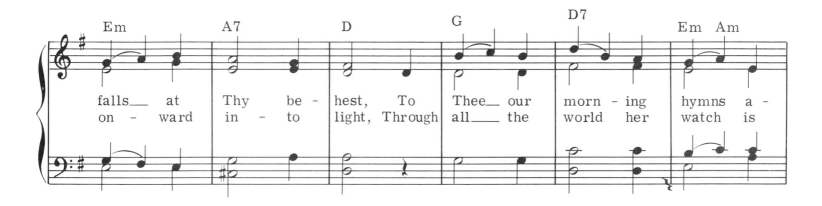

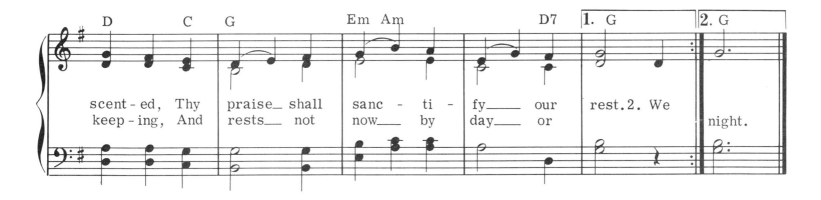

3. As o'er each continent and island
   The dawn leads on to another day,
   The voice of prayer is never silent,
   Nor dies the strain of praise away.

4. The sun that bids us rest is waking
   Our brethren 'neath the western sky,
   And hour by hour fresh lips are making
   Thy wondrous doings heard on high.

5. So be it, Lord: Thy throne shall never
   Like earth's proud empires, pass away;
   Thy Kingdom stands and grows forever
   Till all Thy creatures own Thy sway.

Dear Lord and Father Of Mankind

4. Drop thy still dews of quientness,
   Till all our strivings cease:
   Take from our souls the strain and stress,
   And let our ordered lives confess
   The beauty of thy peace.

5. Breathe through the heats of our desire
   Thy coolness and thy balm;
   Let sense be dumb, let flesh retire;
   Speak through the earthquake, wind and fire,
   O still, small voice of calm.

Evening Prayer

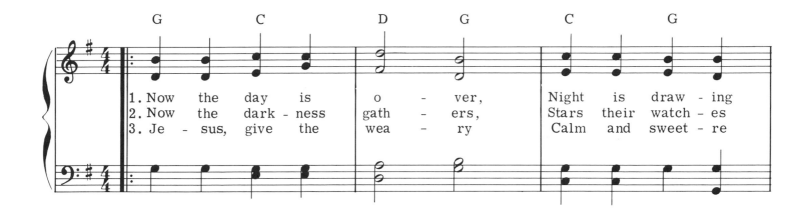

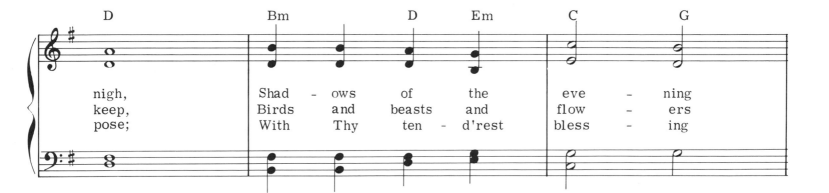

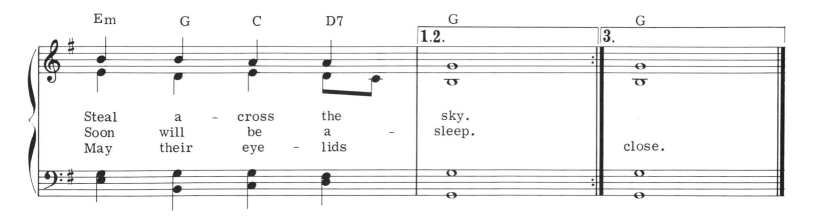

4. Grant to little children	5. Through the long nightwatches	6. When the morning wakens,
Visions bright of Thee	May Thine angels spread	Then may I arise
Guard the sailors tossing	Their white wings above me,	Pure and fresh and sinless,
On the angry sea.	Watching round my bed.	In Thy holy eyes.

Fairest Lord Jesus

1. Fair - est Lord Je - sus, Rul - er of all na - ture,
2. Fair are the mead - ows, Fair - er still the wood - lands,
3. Fair is the sun - shine, Fair - er still the moon - light,

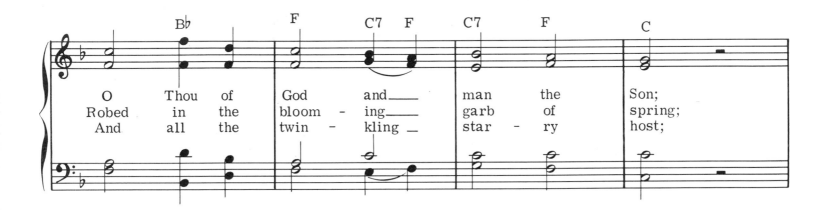

O Thou of God and____ man the Son;
Robed in the bloom - ing____ garb of spring;
And all the twin - kling _ star - ry host;

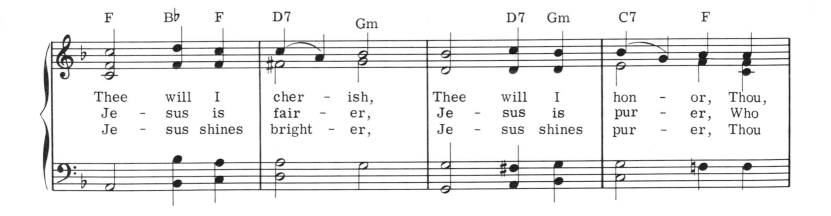

Thee will I cher - ish, Thee will I hon - or, Thou,
Je - sus is fair - er, Je - sus is pur - er, Who
Je - sus shines bright - er, Je - sus shines pur - er, Thou

my soul's glo - ry, joy and crown.
makes the woe - ful heart to sing.
all the an - gels heav'n can boast.

Father, We Thank Thee For The Night

1. Fa - ther, we thank Thee for the__ night, And for the pleas - ant
2. Help us to do the things we__ should, To be to oth - ers

morn - ing light; For rest and food and lov - ing__ care,
kind__ and good; In all we do, in work or__ play,

And all that makes the__ world so__ fair.
To grow more lov - ing__

ev - 'ry__ day.

Gentle Jesus, Meek And Mild

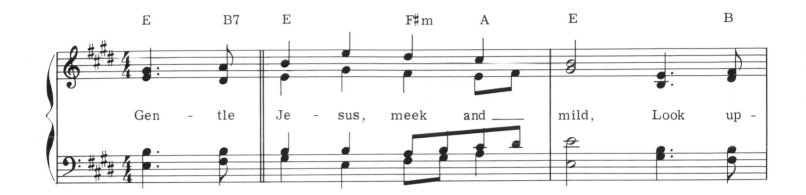

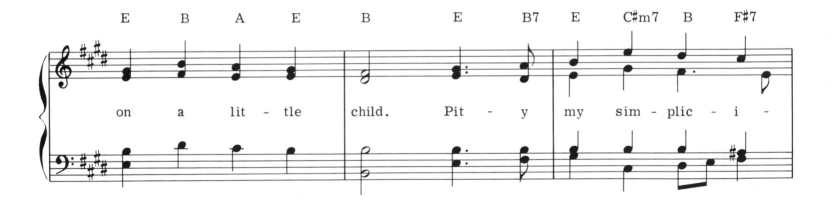

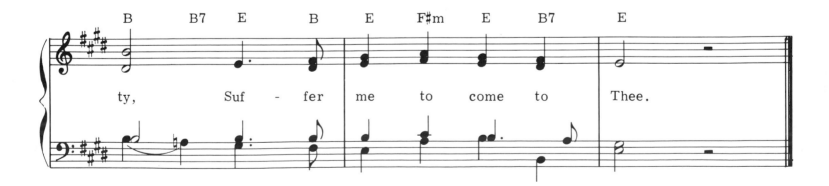

A Child's Grace

Thank you for the world so sweet,
Thank you for the food we eat,
Thank you for the birds that sing —
Thank you, God, for everything.

Glorious Things Of Thee Are Spoken

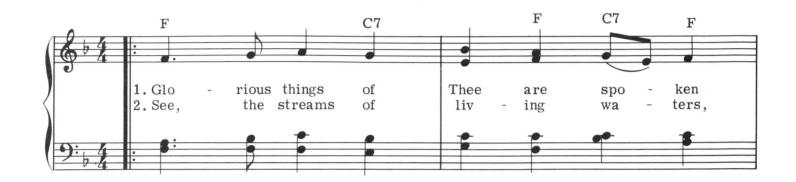

1. Glo - rious things of Thee are spo - ken
2. See, the streams of liv - ing wa - ters,

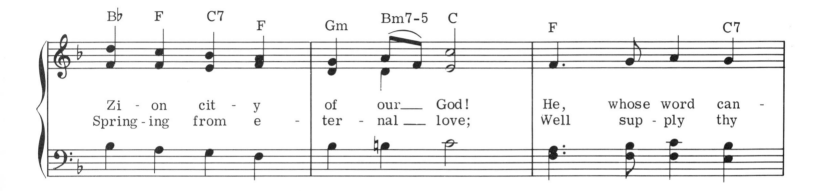

Zi - on cit - y of our___ God! He, whose word can
Spring - ing from e - ter - nal ___ love; Well sup - ply thy

not be bro - ken Formed thee for His own a - bode.
sons and daugh - ters, And all for fear of want re - move.

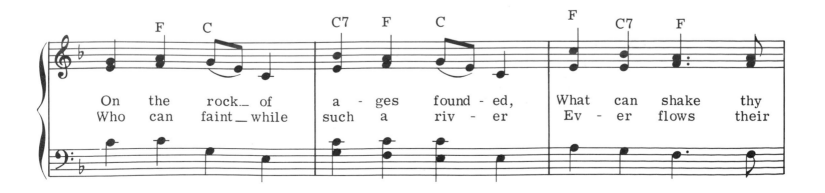

On the rock___ of a - ges found - ed, What can shake thy
Who can faint ___ while such a riv - er Ev - er flows their

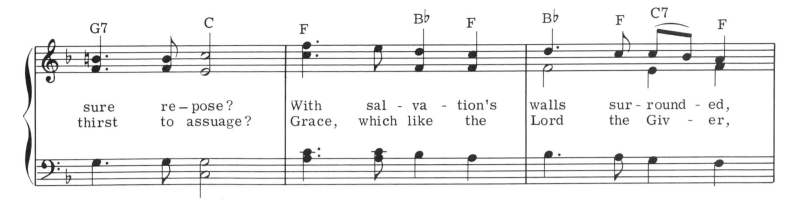

sure   re-pose?
thirst   to assuage?

With   sal - va - tion's
Grace,   which like   the

walls   sur - round - ed,
Lord   the Giv - er,

Thou   may'st smile - at   all   thy foes.
Nev - er   fails - from

1. ... 2. age   to   age.

3. Round each habitation hov'ring,
   See the cloud and fire appear
   For a glory and a cov'ring
   Showing that the Lord is near.
   Thus they march, the pillar leading,
   Light by night and shade by day;
   Daily on the manna feeding
   Which He gives them when they pray.

4. Savior, if or Zion's city
   I, through grace, a member am,
   Let the world deride or pity,
   I will glory in Thy name:
   Fading is the worldling's pleasure,
   All his boasted pomp and show;
   Solid joys and lasting treasure
   None but Zion's children know.

God Of The Earth, The Sky, The Sea

God Of The Glorious Sunshine

1. God of the glo-rious sun - shine, God of re-fresh-ing rain,___ Whose voice bids_ earth a - wak - en And clothe it - self a - gain. With life of_ rich-est beau - ty In plant, in flow'r, and tree, Thou God of_ light and splen - dor, We rise and_ wor-ship Thee.

2. God of the hill and moun-tain, Of val-ley and of dale,___ Whose fin - ger_ paints the rain - bows; Thy beau-ties nev - er fail To raise our_ souls in won - der, And turn our thoughts to Thee; Thou God of_ liv - ing na - ture We stand and_ wor-ship thee.

3. God of the busy daytime,
God of the quiet night,
Whose peace pervades the darkness
And greets us with the light,
Safe with thy presence near us,
Wherever we may be,
Thou God, our great Protector,
We love and worship Thee.

4. God of the whole creation,
God of all life below,
We seek thy nearest presence,
Thy grander life to know;
When we, thy heightened splendor,
Thy greater glories see,
Thou God of all creation,
We still shall worship Thee.

God, That Madest Earth And Heaven

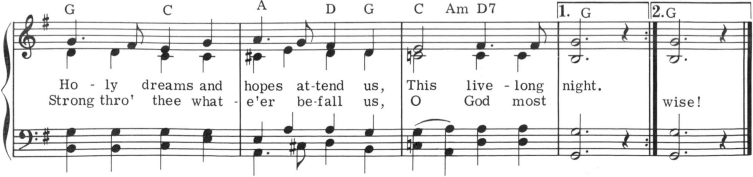

Holy, Holy, Holy

2. Holy, holy, holy! all the saints adore Thee,
   Casting down their golden crowns around the glassy sea,
   Cherubim and seraphim, falling down before Thee,
   Who wert and art, and evermore shalt be.

3. Holy, holy, holy! though the darkness hide Thee,
   Though the eye of sinful man Thy glory may not see,
   Only Thou art holy, there is none beside Thee
   Perfect in power, in love and purity.

4. Holy, holy, holy! Lord God Almighty!
   All Thy works shall praise Thy name, in earth and sky and sea:
   Holy, holy, holy! merciful and mighty!
   God in three Persons, blessed trinity!

How Firm The Foundation

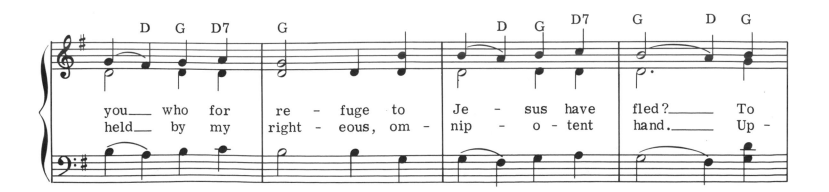

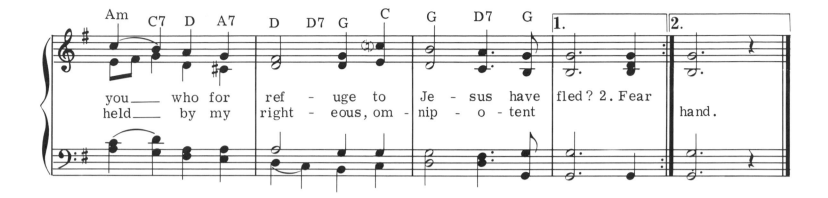

you___ who for | ref - uge to | Je - sus have | fled ? 2. Fear |
held___ by my | right - eous, om - | nip - o -tent | | hand.

3. When through the deep waters
    I call thee to go,
The rivers of sorrow
    shall not overflow;
For I will be with thee,
    thy troubles to bless,
And sanctify to thee
    thy deepest distress,

4. The soul that on Jesus
    hath leaned for repose,
I will not, I will not
    desert to his foes;
That soul, tho' all hell should
    endeavor to shake,
I'll never, no, never,
    no, never forsake.

How Great Thou Art

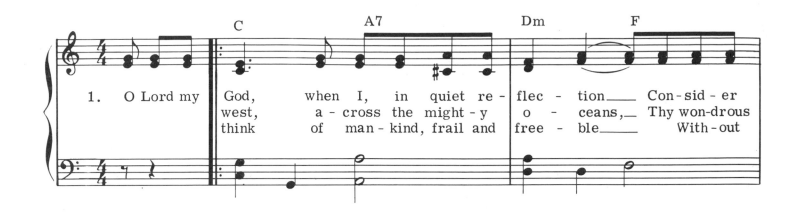

1. O Lord my God, when I, in quiet re - flec - tion___ Con - sid - er
west, a - cross the might - y o - ceans,___ Thy won - drous
think of man - kind, frail and free - ble___ With - out

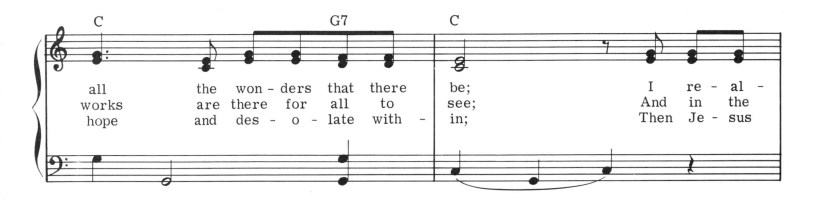

all the won - ders that there be; I re - al -
works are there for all to see; And in the
hope and des - o - late with - in; Then Je - sus

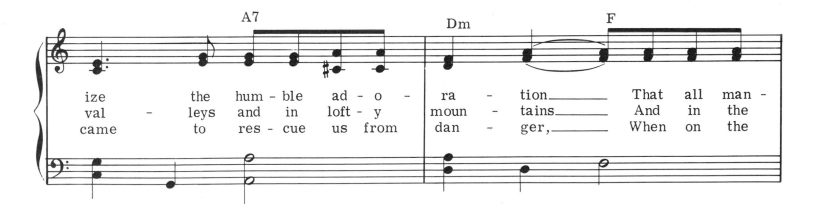

ize the hum - ble ad - o - ra - tion___ That all man -
val - leys and in loft - y moun - tains___ And in the
came to res - cue us from dan - ger,___ When on the

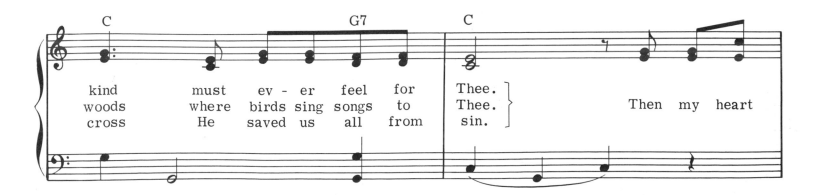

kind must ev - er feel for Thee.
woods where birds sing songs to Thee.
cross He saved us all from sin.
Then my heart

fills   with glow - ing love for   Thee.   How   great Thou

art!   How great Thou art!   Then my heart fills   with glow-ing love for

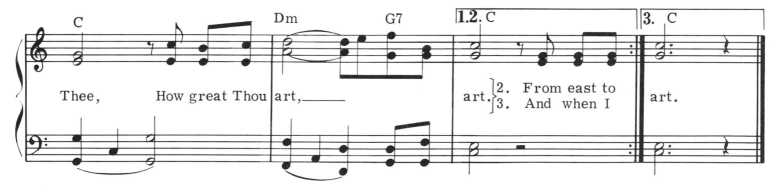

Thee,   How great Thou art,____   art. { 2. From east to
                                                                 { 3. And when I   art.

I Love To Tell The Story

3. I love to tell the story;
   'Tis pleasant to repeat
   What seems, each time I tell it,
   More wonderfully sweet.
   I love to tell the story,
   For some have never heard
   The message of salvation,
   From God's own holy Word.

4. I love to tell the story;
   For those who know it best
   Seem hungering and thirsting
   To hear it, like the rest.
   And when in scenes of glory,
   I sing the new, new song,
   It will be the old, old story,
   That I have loved so long.

I Would Be True

1. I would be true, for there are those who trust me;
2. I would be - friend of all the foe, the friend - less;

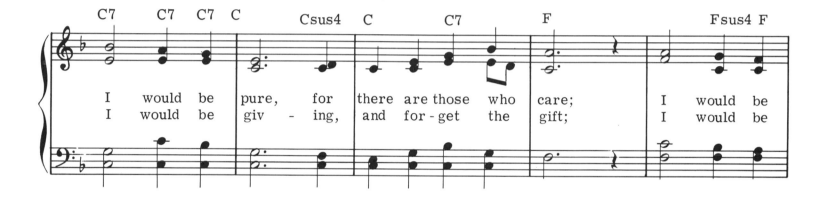

I would be pure, for there are those who care; I would be
I would be giv - ing, and for - get the gift; I would be

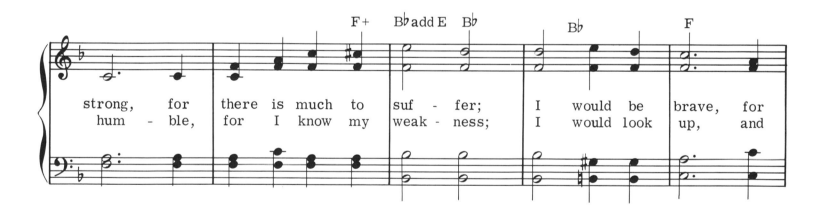

strong, for there is much to suf - fer; I would be brave, for
hum - ble, for I know my weak - ness; I would look up, and

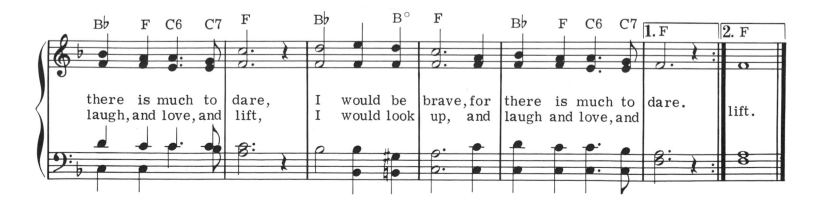

there is much to dare, I would be brave, for there is much to dare.
laugh, and love, and lift, I would look up, and laugh and love, and lift.

Jesus Loves Me! This I Know

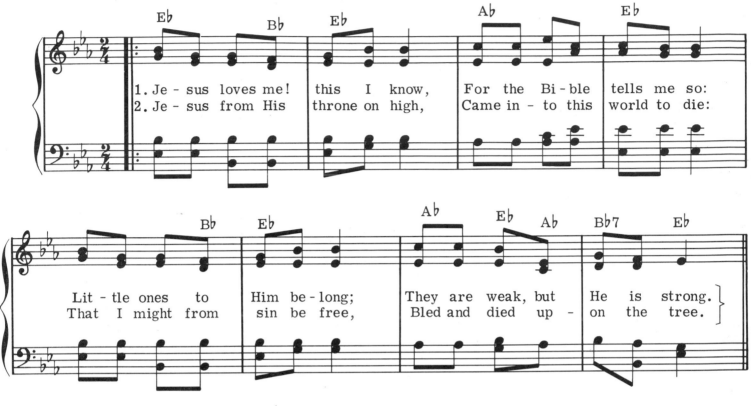

1. Je - sus loves me! this I know, For the Bi - ble tells me so:
2. Je - sus from His throne on high, Came in - to this world to die:

Lit - tle ones to Him be - long; They are weak, but He is strong.
That I might from sin be free, Bled and died up - on the tree.

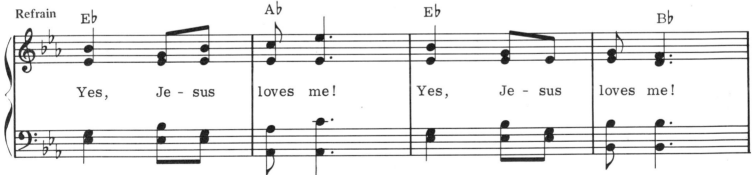

Refrain

Yes, Je - sus loves me! Yes, Je - sus loves me!

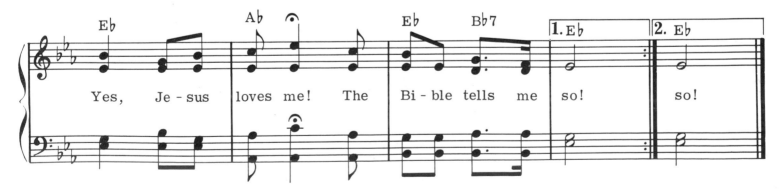

Yes, Je - sus loves me! The Bi - ble tells me so! so!

3. Jesus! loves me! He who died
   Heaven's gates to open wide,
   He will wash away my sin,
   Let His little child come in.

4. Jesus, take this heart of mine;
   Make it pure, and wholly Thine:
   Thou has bled and died for me,
   I will henceforth live for Thee.

Jesus Tender Shepherd, Hear Me

Jesus Wants Me For A Sunbeam

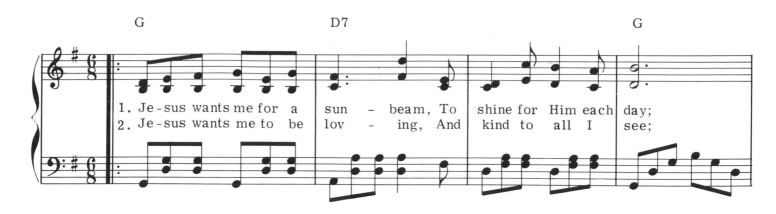

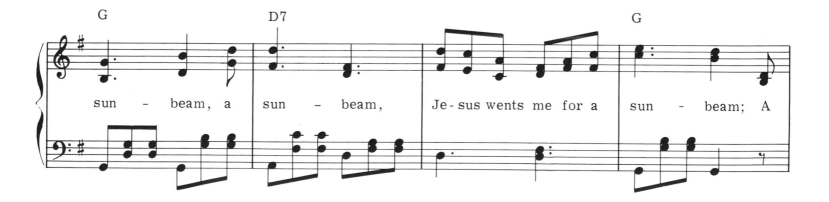

Lead Kindly Light

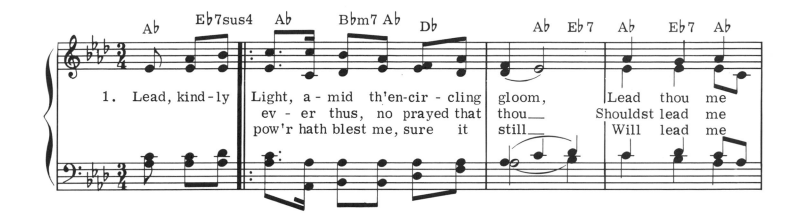

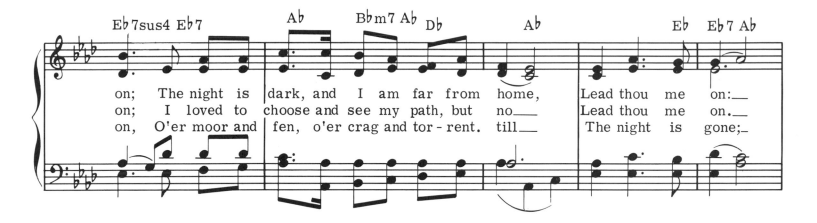

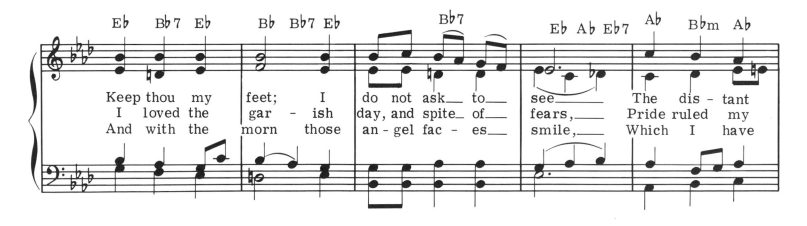

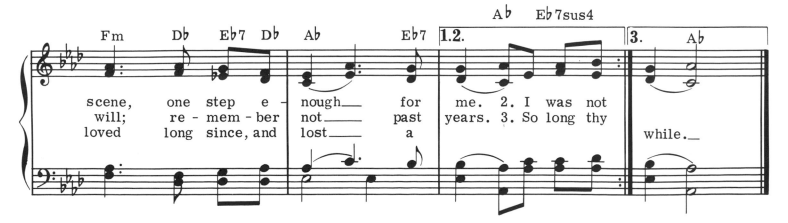

Lead Us Heavenly Father

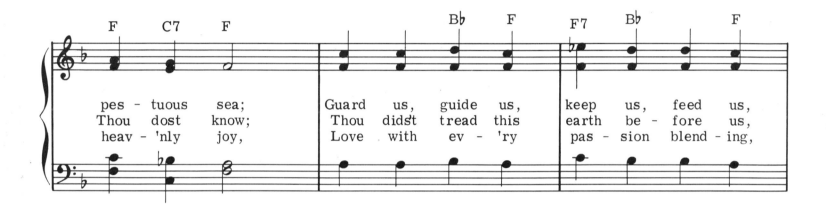

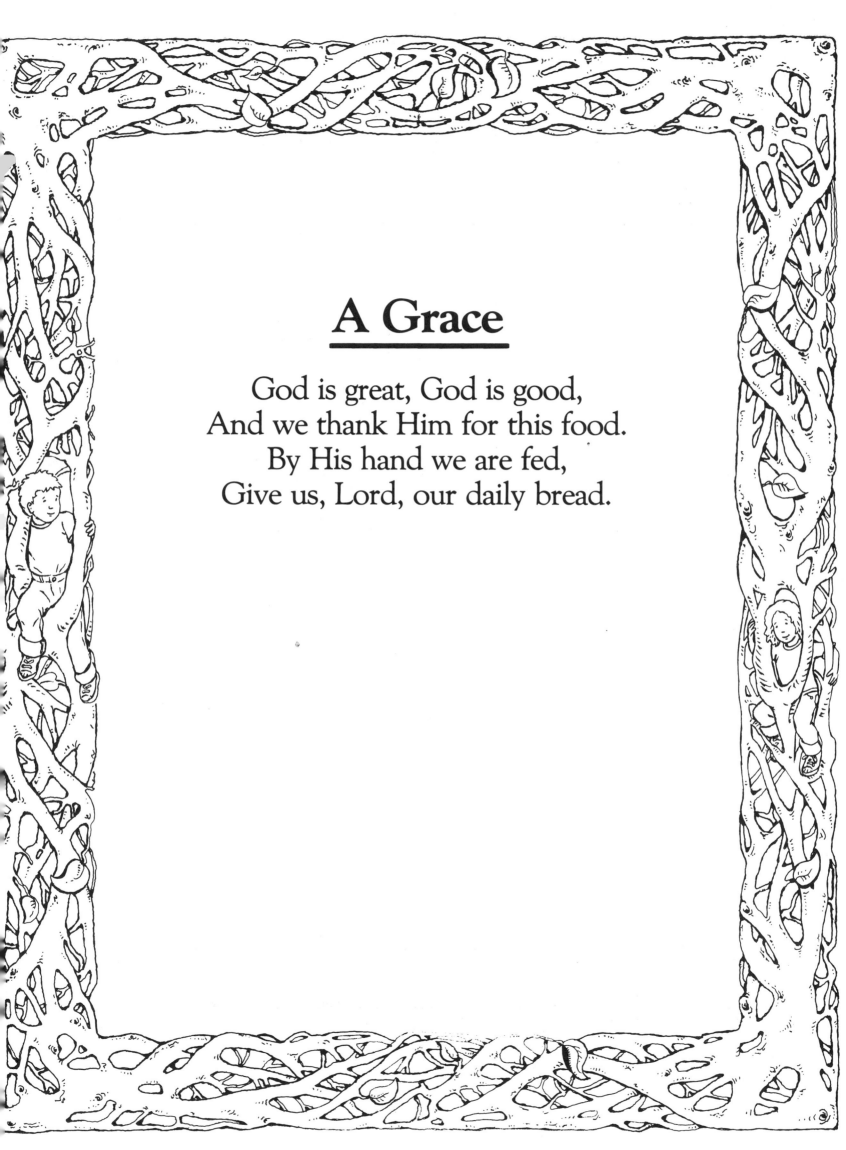

A Grace

God is great, God is good,
And we thank Him for this food.
By His hand we are fed,
Give us, Lord, our daily bread.

A Mighty Fortress Is Our God

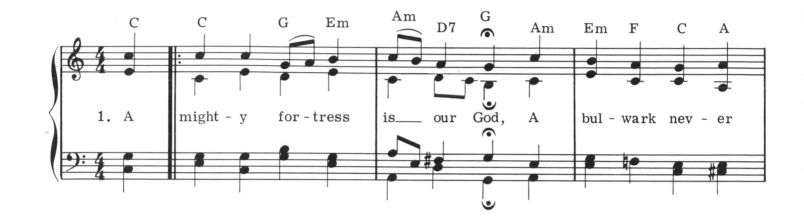

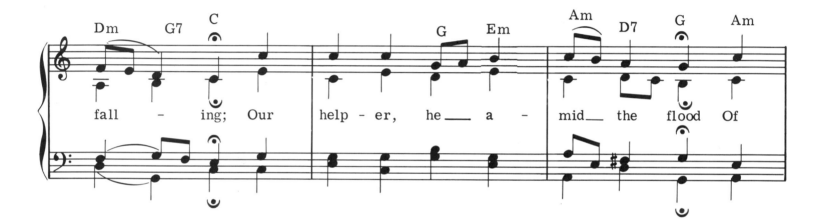

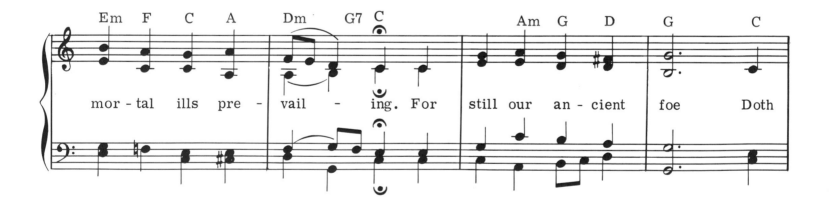

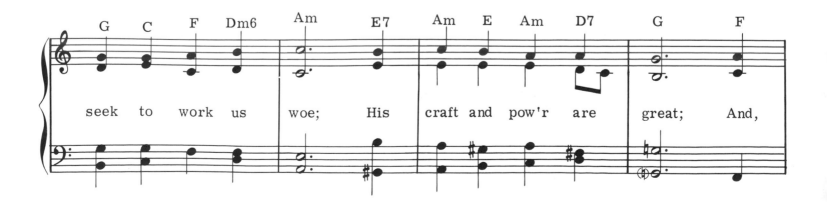

armed with cru - el hate, On earth is not his e - qual.

2. Did we in our own strength confide,
   Our striving would be losing;
   Were not the right man on our side,
   The man of God's own choosing.
   Dost ask who that may be?
   Christ Jesus, it is he,
   Lord Sabaoth his name,
   From age to age the same,
   And he must win the battle.

3. And tho' this world, with devils filled,
   Should threaten to undo us;
   We will not fear, for God hath willed
   His truth to triumph through us.
   The Prince of darkness grim,
   We tremble not for him;
   His rage we can endure,
   For lo, his doom is sure,
   One little word shall fell him.

4. That word above all earthly powers,
   No thanks to them, abideth;
   The Spirit and the gifts are ours
   Thro' him who with us sideth.
   Let goods and kindred go,
   The mortal life also;
   The body they may kill;
   God's truth abideth still,
   His Kingdom is forever.

Mine Eyes Have Seen The Glory

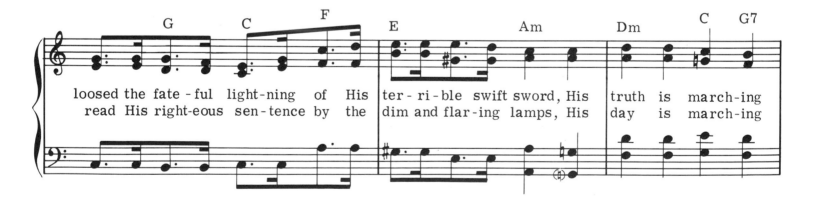

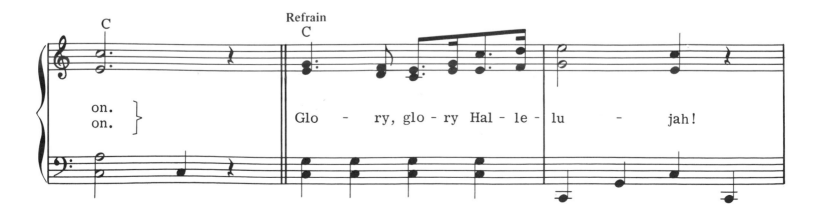

3. I have read a fiery gospel
      writ in burnished rows of steel,
   "As ye deal with My contemner,
      so with you My grace will deal!"
   Let the hero born of woman
      crush the serpent with His heel,
   Since God is marching on.

      (Refrain)

4. He hath sounded forth the trumpet
      that shall never call retreat,
   He is sifting out the hearts of men
      before His judgment seat;
   O, be swift, my soul, to answer Him:
      be jubilent, my feet!
   Our God is marching on.

      (Refrain)

5. In the beauty of the lilies
      Christ was born, across the sea,
   With a glory in His bosom
      that transfigures you and me;
   As He died to make men holy,
      let us live to make men free,
   While God is marching on.

      (Refrain)

O God Our Help

1. O God our help in ages past, Our hope for years to come, Our shelter from the storm-y blast, And our e-ter-nal home.

Un-der the shad-ow of Thy throne, Thy saints have dwelt se-cure; Suf-fi-cient is Thine arm a-lone And our de-fense is sure.

Be-fore the hills in or-der stood, Or earth re-ceived her frame, From ev-er-last-ing Thou art God, To end-less years the same.

4. A thousand ages in Thy sight
   Are like an evening gone,
   Short as the watch that ends the night
   Before the rising sun.

5. Time, like an ever-rolling stream,
   Bears all its song away,
   They fly forgotten, as a dream
   Dies at the opening day.

6. O God our help in ages past,
   Our hope for years to come
   Be Thou our guard while troubles last
   And our eternal home.

Evening Prayer

Now I lay me down to sleep,
I pray the Lord my soul to keep.
God be with me through the night,
And bless me with the morning light.

O Worship The King

1. O wor - ship the King, all glo - rious a - bove, O
   tell of His might, O sing of His grace, Whose
   earth with its store of won - ders un - told, Al -

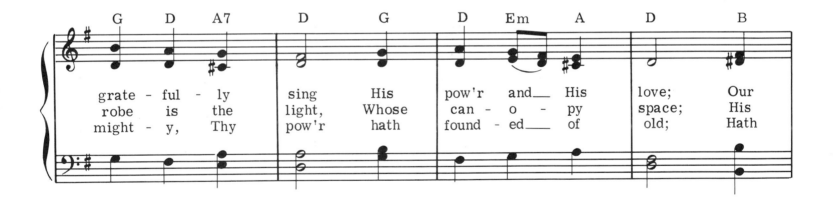

grate - ful - ly sing His pow'r and___ His love; Our
robe is the light, Whose can - o - py space; His
might - y, Thy pow'r hath found - ed___ of old; His

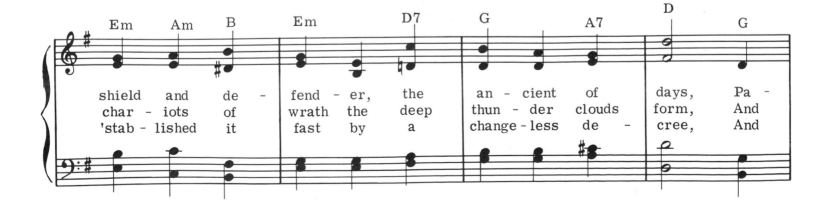

shield and de - fend - er, the an - cient of days, Pa - And
char - iots of wrath the deep thun - der clouds form, And
'stab - lished it fast by a change - less de - cree, And

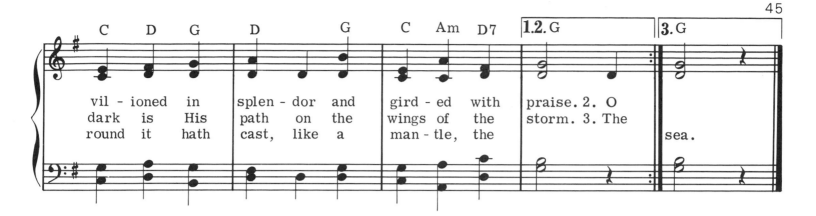

| C | D | G | D | G | C | Am | D7 | **1.2.** G | **3.** G |

vil - ioned   in   splen - dor and   gird - ed with   praise. 2. O
dark is   His   path   on   the   wings of   the   storm. 3. The
round it   hath   cast, like   a   man - tle,   the   sea.

4. Thy bountiful care what tongue can recite?
    It breathes in the air, it shines in the light;
    It streams from the hills, it descends to the plain,
    And sweetly distils in the dew and the rain.

5. Frail children of dust and feeble as frail,
    In Thee do we trust, nor find Thee to fail;
    Thy mercies how tender, how firm to the end,
    Our Maker, Defender, Redeemer and Friend.

6. O measureless Might, ineffable Love,
    While angels delight to hymn Thee above,
    Thy humbler creation, though feeble their lays,
    With true adoration shall sing to Thy praise.

The Old-Time Religion

1. 'Tis the old-time re-li-gion, 'Tis the old-time re-
good for our moth-ers, It was good for our

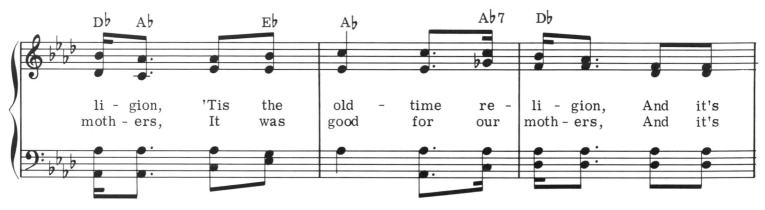

li-gion, 'Tis the old-time re-li-gion, And it's
moth-ers, It was good for our moth-ers, And it's

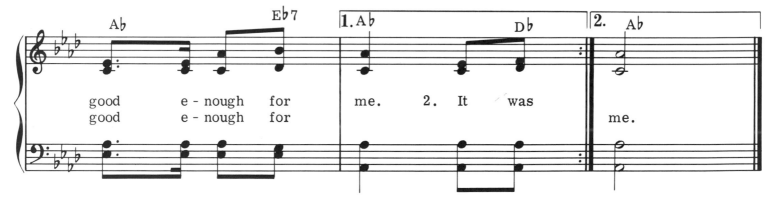

good e-nough for me. 2. It was
good e-nough for me.

3. It has saved our fathers,
   It has saved our fathers,
   It has saved our fathers,
   And it's good enough for me.

4. It was good for the Prophet Daniel,
   It was good for the Prophet Daniel,
   It was good for the Prophet Daniel,
   And it's good enough for me.

5. It was good for the Hebrew children,
   It was good for the Hebrew children,
   It was good for the Hebrew children,
   And it's good enough for me.

6. It was tried in the fiery furnace,
   It was tried in the fiery furnace,
   It was tried in the fiery furnace,
   And it's good enough for me.

7. It will take us all to heaven,
   It will take us all to heaven,
   It will take us all to heaven,
   And it's good enough for me.

The Lord's Prayer

Our Father, who art in heaven,
Hallowed be Thy Name.
Thy Kingdom come, Thy will be done on earth
as it is in heaven.
Give us this day our daily bread, and
forgive us our trespasses,
As we forgive those who trespass against us.
And lead us not into temptation, but
deliver us from evil.
For thine is the kingdom, the power, and the glory,
For ever, and ever.
Amen.

48

Onward Christian Soldiers

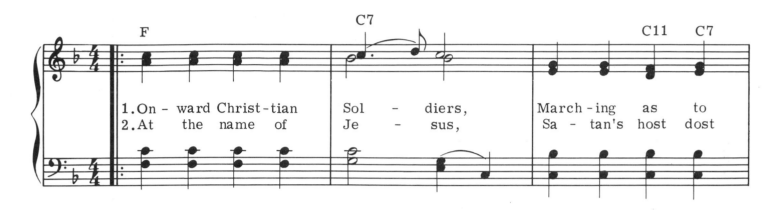

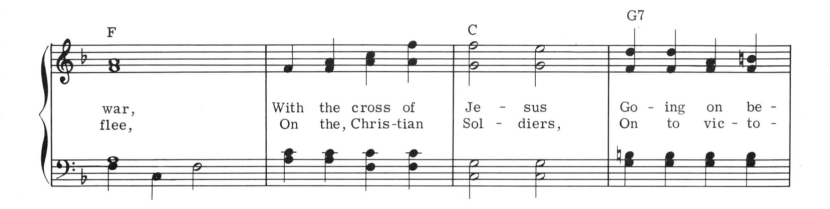

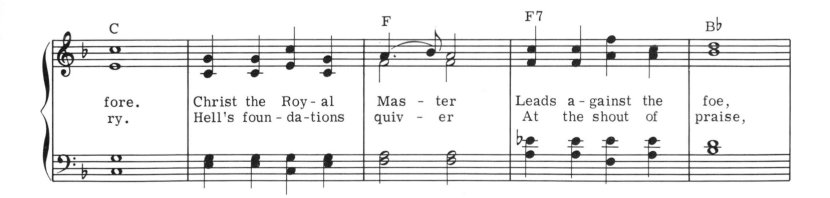

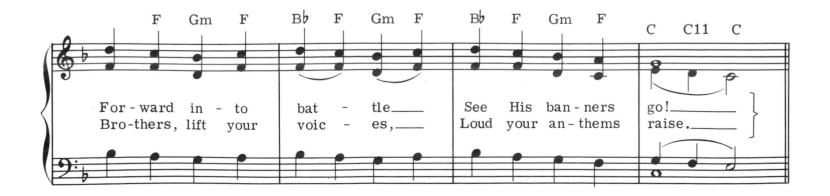

3. Like a mighty army
   Moves the Church of God.
   Brothers, we are treading
   Where the saints have trod.
   We are not divided,
   All one body we,
   One in hope and purpose,
   One in charity.

   (Refrain)

4. Crowns and thrones may perish,
   Kingdoms rise and wane,
   But the Church of Jesus
   Constant will remain:
   Gates of hell can never
   'Gainst that Church prevail;
   We have Christ's own promise
   And that cannot fail.

   (Refrain)

5. Onward then, ye people,
   Join our happy throng,
   Blend with ours your voices
   In the triumph song:
   "Glory, praise and honor
   Unto Christ the King!"
   This through countless ages
   Men and angels sing.

   (Refrain)

Praise Him, All Ye Little Children

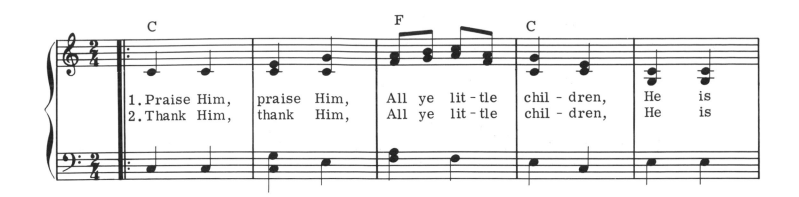

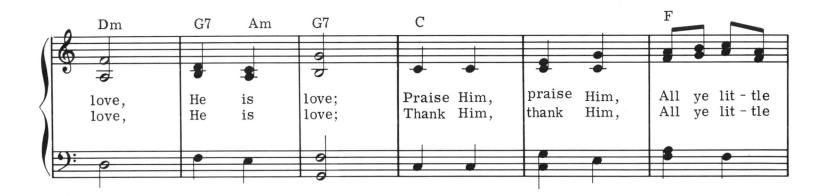

3. Love Him, love Him,
   All ye little children,
   He is love,
   He is love,
   Love Him, love Him,
   All ye little children,
   He is love,
   He is love.

4. Crown Him, crown Him,
   All ye little children,
   He is love,
   He is love;
   Crown Him, crown Him,
   All ye little children,
   He is love,
   He is love.

Shepherd Of Tender Youth

1. Shep-herd of ten - der youth, Guid - ing in love and truth, Through de - vious ways; Christ, our tri-umph-ant King, We come thy name to sing; Hith - er our chil - dren bring To sound Thy praise.

2. Thou art our ho - ly Lord, The all sub-du - ing Word, Heal - er of strife; Thou didst thy-self a - base, That from sin's deep dis - grace Thou might-est save our race, And give us life.

3. Ever be Thou our guide,
Our Shepherd and our pride,
Our staff and song;
Jesus, Thou Christ of god,
By Thy perennial word,
Lead us where Thou hast trod,
Make our faith strong.

4. So now, and till we die,
Sound we Thy praises high,
And joyful sing;
Let all the holy throng
Who To Thy church belong,
Unite and swell the song
To Christ, our King.

Silent Night

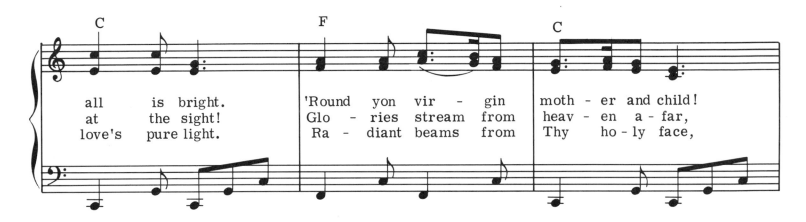

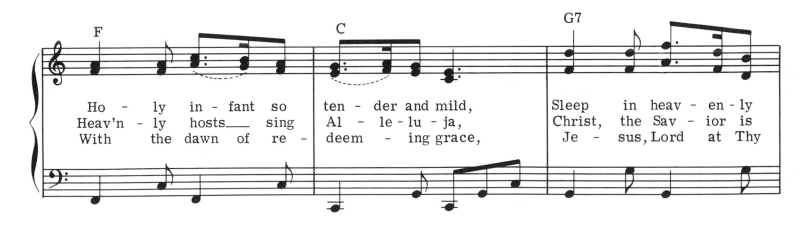

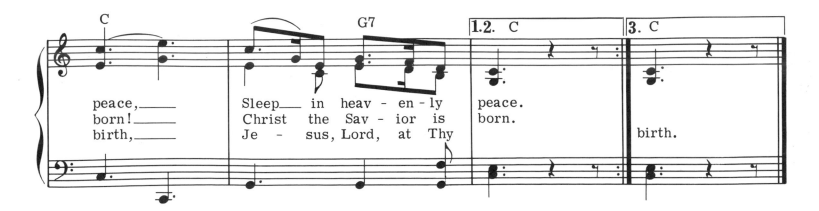

Sing Hosanna

1. Give me joy in my heart, keep me praising, ___ Give me joy in my heart, I
   peace in my heart, keep me rest-ing, ___ Give me peace in my heart, I
   love in my heart, keep me serv-ing, ___ Give me love in my heart, I

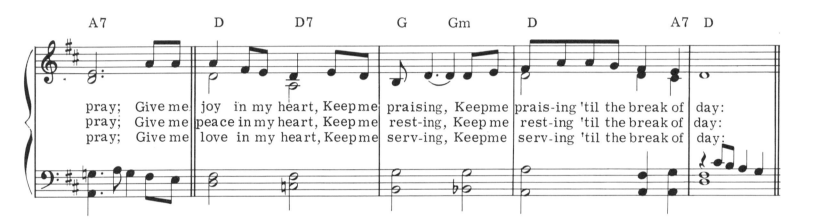

pray; Give me joy in my heart, Keep me praising, Keep me prais-ing 'til the break of day:
pray; Give me peace in my heart, Keep me rest-ing, Keep me rest-ing 'til the break of day:
pray; Give me love in my heart, Keep me serv-ing, Keep me serv-ing 'til the break of day:

chorus

Sing Ho-san-na! Sing Ho-san-na! Sing Ho-san-na to the King of Kings!

Sing Ho-san-na! Sing Ho-san-na! Sing Ho-san-na to the King! 2. Give me
3. Give

King!

Stand Up, Stand Up For Jesus

3. Stand up, stand up for Jesus,
   Stand in His strength alone'
   The arm of flesh will fail you,
   Ye dare not trust your own.
   Put on the gospel armor,
   Each piece put on with prayer;
   Where duty calls, or danger,
   Be never wanting there.

4. Stand up, stand up for Jesus,
   The strife will not be long;
   This day the noise of battle,
   The next the victor's song
   To him that overcometh
   A crown of life shall be;
   He with the King of Glory
   Shall reign eternally.

There Is A Green Hill

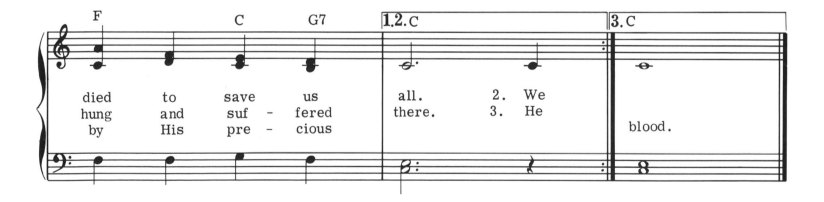

4. There was no other good enough
   To pay the price of sin;
   He only could unlock the gate
   Of Heaven, and let us in.

5. O dearly, dearly has He loved,
   And we must love Him too,
   And trust in His redeeming blood;
   And try His words to do.

There's A Friend For Little Children

1. There's a Friend for lit - tle chil - dren A - bove the bright blue

sky; _____ A Friend who nev - er chang - es, Whose love can nev - er

die. _____ Un - like our friends by na - ture, Who change with chang - ing

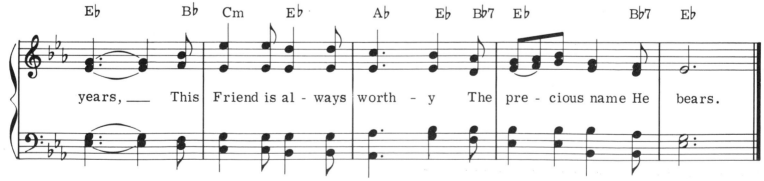

years, __ This Friend is al - ways worth - y The pre - cious name He bears.

2. There's a song for little children
Above the bright blue sky,

A song that will not weary
Though sung continually;

A song which even angels
Can never, never sing;

They know not Christ as Savior,
But worship Him as King.

3. There's robe for little children
Above the bright blue sky,

And a harp of sweetest music,
And a plan of victory.

All, all above is treasured,
And found in Christ alone;

O come, dear little children,
That all may be your own.

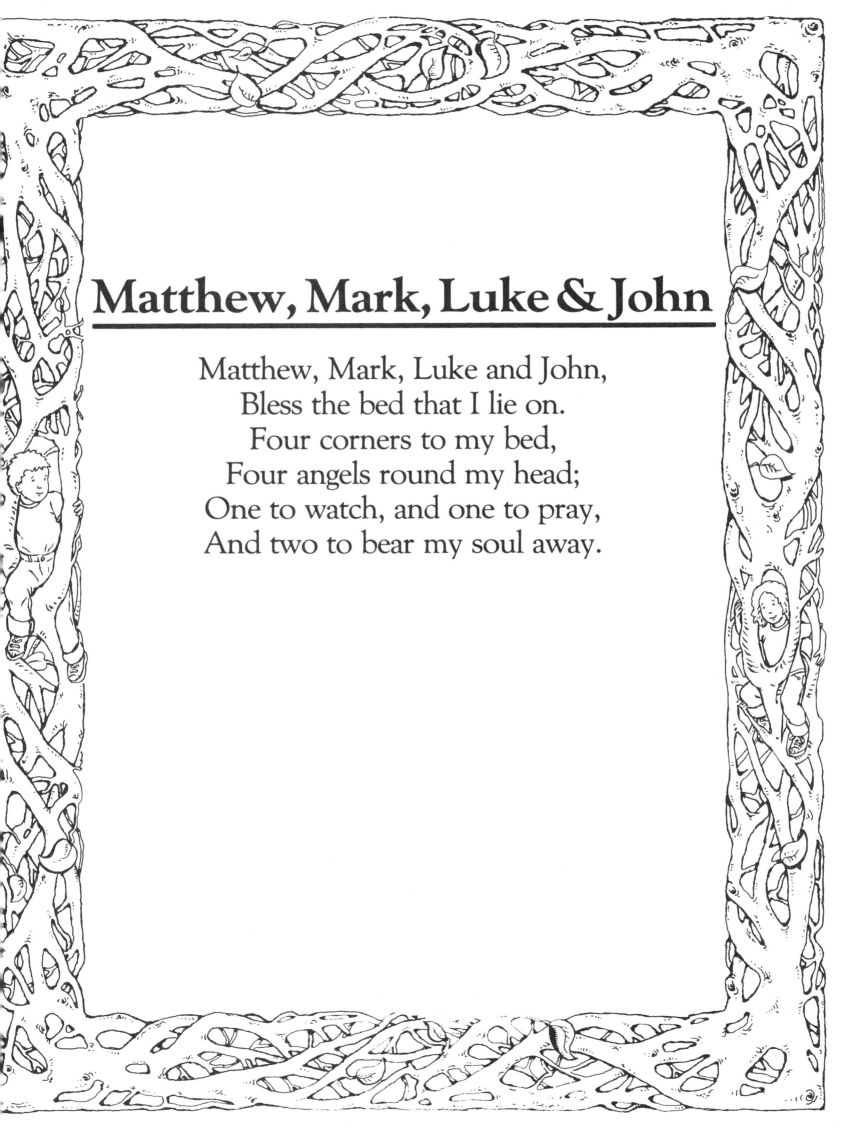

Matthew, Mark, Luke & John

Matthew, Mark, Luke and John,
Bless the bed that I lie on.
Four corners to my bed,
Four angels round my head;
One to watch, and one to pray,
And two to bear my soul away.

We Plough The Fields

breez - es, and the | sun - shine, And | soft re - fresh - ing
more to us, His | chil - dren, He | gives one dai - ly
what Thou most de - | sir - est, Our | hum - ble thank - ful

rain.
bread.
hearts.
All good gifts a - round us Are

sent from heav'n a - bove; Then thank the Lord, O

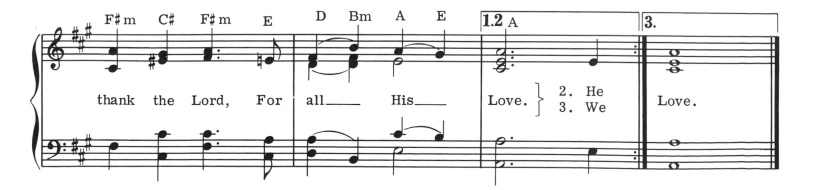

thank the Lord, For all___ His___ Love.

2. He
3. We

Love.

Thank You, God

God made the sun
And God made the tree,
God made the mountains
And God made me.

I thank you, O God,
For the sun and the tree,
For making the mountains
And for making me.

Thank You Prayer

Thank You for the world so bright.
Thank You for the warm sunlight.
Thank You for the stars above.
Thank You for Your endless love.

What A Friend We Have In Jesus

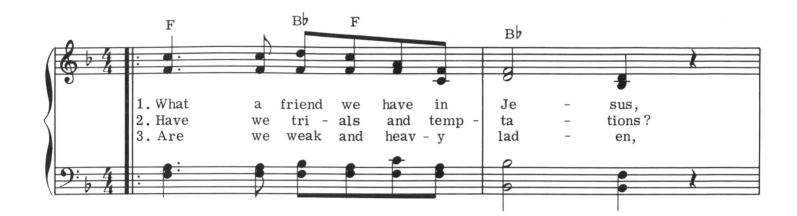

1. What a friend we have in Je - sus,
2. Have we tri - als and temp - ta - tions?
3. Are we weak and heav - y lad - en,

All our sins and griefs to | bear! What a priv - i - lege to
Is there trou - ble an - y - | where? We should nev - er be dis -
Cum - bered with a load of | care? Pre - cious Sav - ior, still our

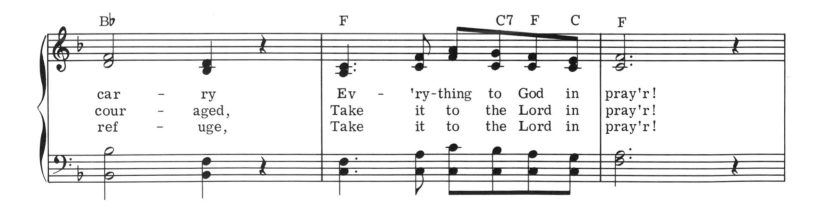

car - ry | Ev - 'ry-thing to God in | pray'r!
cour - aged, | Take it to the Lord in | pray'r!
ref - uge, | Take it to the Lord in | pray'r!

O what peace we of - ten | for - feit, O what need-less pain we
Can we find a friend so | faith - ful Who will all our sor - rows
Do thy friends de-spise, for - | sake thee? Take it to the Lord in

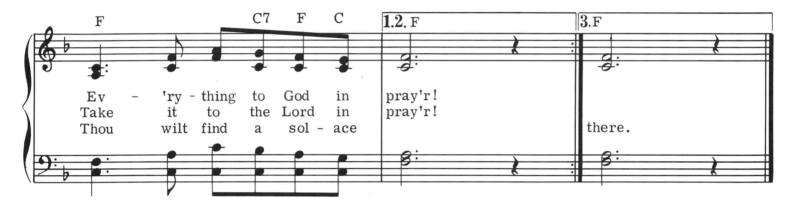

bear. All be - cause we do not car - ry
share? Je - sus knows our ev - 'ry weak - ness;
pray'r! In His arms He'll take and shield thee;

Ev - 'ry - thing to God in pray'r!
Take it to the Lord in pray'r!
Thou wilt find a sol - ace there.

23rd Psalm

The Lord is my shepherd; I shall not want.
He maketh me to lie down in green pastures: He
leadeth me beside the still waters.
He restoreth my soul: He leadth me in path of
righteousness for His name's sake.
Yea, though I walk through the valley of the shadow
of death, I will fear no evil: for Thou art with me;
Thy rod and Thy staff, they comfort me.
Thou preparest a table before me in the presence of
mine enemies. Thou anointest my head with oil;
my cup runneth over.
Surely goodness and mercy shall follow me all the
days of my life: and I will dwell in the house of
the Lord for ever.